RHINOS

Acknowledgments
Thanks to KZN Wildlife, Mark Cooke, Sunil Borah and Dr Sen Nathan

Text and photographs © 2002 by Ann and Steve Toon
except: page 13 top © 2002 Alain Compost / Still Pictures
page 13 below © 2002 Mella Panzella / Oxford Scientific Films

Printed in China

02 03 04 05 06   5 4 3 2 1

Library of Congress Cataloging-in-Publication Data available

ISBN 0-89658-586-7

Distributed in Canada by Raincoast Books, 9050 Shaughnessy Street, Vancouver, B.C. V6P 6E5

Published by Voyageur Press, Inc.
123 North Second Street, P.O. Box 338, Stillwater, MN 55082 U.S.A.
651-430-2210, fax 651-430-2211
books@voyageurpress.com
www.voyageurpress.com

Educators, fundraisers, premium and gift buyers, publicists, and marketing managers:
Looking for creative products and new sales ideas? Voyageur Press books are available at special discounts when purchased in quantities, and special editions can be created to your specifications. For details contact the marketing department at 800-888-9653.

RHINOS

Ann and Steve Toon

WorldLife
LIBRARY

Voyageur Press

Contents

Introduction

The rhinoceros is one of the animal world's true heavyweights. Tales of bad-tempered rhinos charging through the bush in a cloud of dust are campfire classics, told to thrill guests on an African safari. That massive, shovel-shaped head, that huge, barrel-like body in its overlarge 'battlejacket', those fearsome horns – a belligerent rhinoceros is not an animal to pick a fight with.

Of the five surviving species, the white rhino and the Indian one-horned rhino, weighing in at well in excess of two tonnes, share the title of largest land mammal after the elephant. Formidable as they are, however, it's not just their bulk and impressive armory that makes them one of the world's most remarkable animals. Our fascination with rhinos has as much to do with the fact that these thickset, thickskinned and ponderous mammals still bear the features of their prehistoric ancestors. Some 60 million years of evolution are encapsulated in that intimidating profile. This visible link to the past, coupled with the very real threat of extinction, has given the rhino a special symbolism.

Working as wildlife photographers, we have had some adrenalin-inducing encounters with rhinos: riding with a game capture team alongside an angry African black rhino as he thundered along, repeatedly crashing into our vehicle until the tranquilizing dart took effect; holding our breath on the back of a swaying elephant as an Indian one-horned rhino confidingly introduced her month-old calf to us; fending off the attentions of a precocious hand-reared white rhino orphan just a few weeks old.

So how many rhinos are left in the wild today? Of the estimated 16,000 rhinos remaining in the world more than 10,000 are white rhino. Theirs is a notable conservation success story resulting in a significant turnaround in the fortunes of this species. But there are fewer than 3000 of Africa's other species, the rare and elusive black rhino, left in the wild, while in Asia there remain fewer than 3000 Indian, Javan and Sumatran rhino in total.

Thrilling encounter – face to face with an Indian one-horned rhino.

The Rhino Family

Origins

Millions of years ago there were numerous species of rhinoceros. Some were as small as sheep, others real giants, much bigger than those we can see in the wild today. Among them was *Indricotherium*, the largest land mammal that ever lived, a rhino half as tall again as an elephant.

Ancestors of the modern rhinoceros even lived in Europe and America. The first traces of horned rhino, living 25 to 40 million years ago, were found in North America. Only a quarter of a million years ago rhinos very much like the modern African species could be found grazing the countryside of southeastern England.

The rhino's closest living relative is the tapir, followed by the horse. All three groups of animals are known as odd-toed ungulates because they have one, three or traces of five toes to each foot. Rhinos have three. They belong to the order of herbivorous mammals called *Perissodactyla*. The rhino family itself is known as *Rhinocerotidae*.

African White Rhino

The most well-known of the five species is the two-horned African white rhino (*Ceratotherium simum*). White rhino are considered to be the most placid and in game parks where these animals have become habituated to tourist vehicles it is possible to approach quite close, unless you encounter a mother with a small calf, when it's advisable to give them plenty of room.

Although the white rhino is now the most numerous species, it nearly became extinct in the early twentieth century. More sociable than other rhinos, it can often be seen grazing in small groups. Confusingly, its common name is not related to its skin color, which can be anything from pale gray to rich, earthy brown, but is thought to come from the Cape Dutch word 'wijdt' meaning wide, as in wide-lipped rhino. This was probably to

The name 'rhinoceros' derives from the Greek, meaning 'nose horn'.

distinguish it from the black rhino, which has a hooked lip.

At home grazing the savannah grasslands of southern and east Africa, today the vast majority of white rhinos live in South Africa, where many rhino conservation techniques were pioneered. Because their numbers continue to increase they are now classified as 'conservation dependent' rather than endangered. A northern subspecies, however, is seriously under threat, with just a handful of wild animals confined to the Garamba National Park in the Democratic Republic of Congo.

African Black Rhino

The two-horned African black, or hook-lipped rhino (*Diceros bicornis*), is a rhino with attitude. It is more aggressive and ill-tempered than its wide-lipped African counterpart, but in spite of its reputation it is a generally shy, secretive animal living in the bushland and savannah of southern and east Africa. Its typical habitat is open rangeland and forest margins. There are four subspecies of black rhino, of which the most common is the southern central subspecies.

South Africa, Namibia, Kenya and Zimbabwe are the key range countries of surviving black rhino populations. There are also around 15 or so black rhino belonging to a rare western subspecies which conservationists are struggling to keep from dying out in Cameroon, west Africa.

Back in the nineteenth century the black rhino was the most numerous of all five species, but numbers declined extremely rapidly in the twentieth century. In just 30 years the population was slashed by as much as 96 per cent, perhaps the fastest decline of any large mammal on record. Since the early 1990s numbers have largely stabilized, but we are still a long way from being in a position to take this species off the endangered list.

Indian One-horned Rhino

Like the African white rhino, the Indian, or Asian greater one-horned rhino (*Rhinoceros unicornis*) boasts a successful conservation record and its numbers have been restored from just a few animals to moderately healthy levels. This species is instantly recognizable

The African black rhino has a reputation for being aggressive but is generally a shy,
solitary and largely nocturnal animal. It is also known as the hook-lipped rhino, with a mouth
shaped like a turtle's beak to enable it to pluck leaves.

because of the huge folds in its skin that look just like armor-plating. Once common throughout the entire northern part of the Indian subcontinent, numbers have declined as a result of hunting, poaching and human encroachment. Today around 2400 remain in the low grasslands and valley swamps of reserves in northeast India and Nepal. Although this rhino has only one small horn, it is still threatened by poachers, particularly as Asian rhino horn is more highly prized than African.

Javan Rhino

The Javan rhino, also known as the Asian lesser one-horned rhino (*Rhinoceros sondaicus*), is not only the rarest of the five species but possibly the rarest large mammal in the world. It is in the same genus as the Indian rhino and wears a similar suit of armor. The Javan rhino lives in tropical rainforest along watercourses, but is so shy that few people get the chance to see it. Once this animal occurred throughout the whole of southeast Asia. There are thought to be only 60 or so left in the wild today, in Indonesia and Vietnam.

Sumatran Rhino

The Sumatran rhino (*Dicerorhinus sumatrensis*) is the smallest of the five species. It is also the only living rhino with a hairy hide. Extremely shy, it is found in the dense, tropical rainforest and mountain forests of peninsula Malaysia, Borneo and Sumatra. There are about 300 left in the wild and these animals are very vulnerable because the population is quite fragmented. Yet in the nineteenth century this animal was so common people considered it a garden pest. It is thought to be a direct descendant of the prehistoric woolly rhino and could be more closely related to the African rhinos than its Asian relatives. Like the two better-known African species, the Sumatran rhino has two horns, a longer one in front and a shorter one behind.

The Javan rhino is possibly the rarest large mammal in the world, with only around 60 left in the wild. Researchers rely on dung and spoor evidence, rather than actual sightings, to study them.

Sumatran rhinos formerly held in zoos are being relocated to enclosures in their natural habitat to encourage them to breed. In September 2001 Cincinnati Zoo had the first successful captive live birth in over 100 years.

Characteristics

It's not hard to see how rhinos earned their place in Africa's big five – elephant, rhino. buffalo, lion and leopard – the most prized and dangerous targets of the trophy hunter. Look at the way they're built to intimidate, with their massive bulk, tough skin, sharp horn and a surprising turn of speed. But appearances can be deceptive. Rhinos might be unpredictable, idiosyncratic, and potentially deadly at times, but they're also surprisingly timid and likely to prefer flight to fight when threatened. A contradictory mix of curiosity and shyness, physical violence plays only a minor role in rhino behavior. Even territorial disputes are more likely to be settled by posturing and diplomacy than by serious fighting.

Anything that crosses a rhino's path still has that formidable presence to contend with, however. The rhino's vertebral column has been likened to a girder, balanced on its forelegs, with the head counterbalancing the body weight, and the hind legs providing the main propulsion. The rhino's short, stumpy legs act like stout pillars to support its huge body weight, while the large, three-toed feet provide firm anchorage on the ground. Rhinos may have the physique of mammals long extinct, but it has proved to be an enduringly successful design. It's no coincidence that while a rhino, as a pure herbivore, is not at the top of the food chain, it has few real predators, apart from man.

Occasionally, rhinos are killed by elephants. This usually happens in disputes over access to water, but has also been known to occur when adolescent bull elephants have been moved to game reserves without the steadying influence of older relatives and start to exhibit abnormal, aggressive behavior patterns. Young rhinos are vulnerable to natural predators such as lions, hyenas or tigers, but are risky prey. Rhinoceros cows might be a little careless when keeping an eye on their calves, but once alerted to danger they put up a formidable defence. Protective mothers have been known to kill lions attempting to take a calf.

Although rhinos have famously poor eyesight, their senses of hearing and smell are

With such a formidable physique rhinos have few predators apart from man.

acute. Disturb a grazing rhino bull and he will lift his head to peer myopically at the source of his annoyance, but watch those ears – large, alert, twitching at every slight sound. Even when sound asleep, eyes tightly closed, a rhino's ears are active, straining to pick up the sound of any advancing intruder.

For added protection rhinos have a few tricks up their sleeve. Oxpeckers, birds that hitch rides on the backs of African rhinos while cleaning ticks from their hides, nose and ears, act as early warning systems, raising the alarm call and taking flight at the approach of danger. African white rhinos and Indian rhinos are often seen grazing in the company of other herbivores, safety in numbers increasing the chance that would-be predators will be spotted.

If danger does threaten, a rhino's first instinct is to make off at a fast trot, head held high and tail curled over its back. Despite their bulk, rhinos are capable of speeds of up to 35 mph (55 kmph), and even a small calf can manage 25 mph (40 kmph). If flight is not an option, then two rhinos may stand with hindquarters together, facing in different directions. Charging an aggressor is usually the last resort of a cornered or surprised rhino, and even then most charges are mock attacks, with the rhino pulling up short. But if a rhinoceros does press home its attack, watch out – that horn is a lethal weapon on the end of two tonnes or more of armor-plated battering ram covering 30 ft (10 meters) per second and able to turn in its own length.

A rhino's horn is more than just a weapon, however, and may be used to clear paths through dense undergrowth, root up vegetation, dig out mineral salts, or break branches off trees to get at food. Rhino horn is made of keratin, similar to compressed hair and fingernails. Although it can have a coarse, hairy appearance near the base, where fraying exposes individual filaments of horn, it's not simply a formation of densely packed hair as is sometimes thought. Higher up, the horn is usually worn smooth. Its exact composition depends on the animal's diet, opening up the intriguing possibility of rhino horn 'fingerprinting', which could allow investigators to identify the source of illegal horn.

Horn tips are very hard, compressed and black, but a piece of horn cut from the middle has a translucent amber glow when held up to light, unfortunately

This curious African black rhino with its poor eyesight cannot see a stationary person at 100 ft (30 m), relying instead on a keen sense of smell and good hearing to detect threats.

White rhinos have the longest horns of all five species and it's possible to see some
fine examples in South African reserves. Sadly, even today rhinos with impressive anterior horns
are sought after by trophy seekers on game farms where hunting is still allowed.

making it an attractive material for ornamental carvings.

Horn grows continually throughout the life of a rhino, though growth is reduced by wear. Growth rates vary, depending on the species, sex and age of the rhino, as well as its environment and behavior. In parts of Africa, conservationists have carried out dehorning programs in an attempt to deter poachers, without any obvious adverse effect on the rhinos' behavior. The horn grows back slowly after removal, so theoretically it would be possible to farm rhino horn by regular 'harvesting'. Dehorning needs to be carried out very carefully, however, because although the horn itself is dead material, nerves and blood vessels are vulnerable to damage.

The biggest horns belong to the white rhino – the longer horn can grow to more than 60 in (150 cm). One pair of trophy horns measured 62 in (158 cm) and 52 in (133 cm). Africa's other rhino species, the black rhino, also has two horns, though in rare cases three have been recorded. Although black rhino are smaller than white rhino, their front horns can still reach an impressive 51 in (130 cm). Asia's only two-horned rhino is the Sumatran species, but this has much smaller horns – the front horn rarely exceeds 12 in (30 cm) and the rear horn is often very small or even missing entirely. Indian and Javan one-horned rhino species have smaller, single horns, usually no more than 6 to 8 in (15 to 20 cm) long.

Heavyweight Herbivores

Rhinos are either grazing animals, like the white rhino, browsers (feeding on shoots, leaves and twigs) like the black rhino, or a combination of the two. Because their food is low in energy they need to keep feeding to stoke their huge appetites, and spend a considerable part of the day and night munching food. Rhinos do not ruminate, but have powerful molars to grind food and a complex gut to digest poor-quality forage. Asian species also have incisors.

The rhino's massive physique means much of its day-to-day life revolves around food. A white rhino male typically weighs up to 4960 lb (2250 kg), and can reach 6600 lb (3000 kg), so getting enough to eat is a time-consuming priority. Feeding occupies at least half of its time, day and night. With poor eyesight, a rhino relies on its sense of smell to find its way round, so can be as active at night as in daylight, especially in hot weather. Rhinos sleep and rest at any time, but will lie up at the hottest part of the day.

Where healthy rhinoceros populations survive, the animal's ecological impact on vegetation and habitat can be quite significant. In South Africa's Hluhluwe-Umfolozi game reserve, for example, white rhinos account for half the biomass of large herbivores and their grazing pressure can convert extensive areas of medium-tall grass to short grasslands.

White rhinos are true grazers, perhaps the largest that have ever lived. They prefer short grass, though their large size allows them to survive on taller, dry grass in times of drought. A white rhino has wide, square lips and a wide muzzle, allowing it to pluck a broad swathe of grass. The upper lip is soft and sensitive for detecting tufts of grass, the lower lip has a hard cutting surface. The powerful muscles needed to hold its over-sized, low-slung head down at ground level for long periods of feeding give the white rhino a pronounced hump between its shoulders.

As a grazing animal, the white rhino was historically restricted to grasslands and savannah. Climatic and vegetation change two million years ago saw the rhino's range split in two, so that today there are geographically and genetically separate northern and southern subspecies.

By contrast, the black rhino, with its more catholic diet, has adapted to a much wider variety of habitats and before human persecution intervened had a correspondingly wider range than the white rhino. Black rhinos are found from deserts to dense forests, and in the past were even recorded on the slopes of Table Mountain, near the southern tip of Africa. Four subspecies of black rhino survive today, each thought to have physiological and behavioral adaptations to specific habitats.

Black rhinos are significantly smaller than white rhinos, with even a big male rarely exceeding 2870 lb (1300 kg). They browse primarily on trees, shrubs and herbaceous

A white rhino eats around 160 lb (72 kg) of grass a day.

plants, but will eat grass when other food is in short supply. More than 200 plant species have been recorded in the black rhino's diet. Small thorn trees and tamboti thickets are their favorite feeding grounds, while in drier times they move into riverine and drainage line habitats. Clumps of bush growing on nutrient-rich termite mounds also provide good eating in the dry season.

The black rhino's mouth is very different to that of a white rhino. Instead of wide, square lips adapted for grazing, it has a turtle-like 'beak', with a mobile, pointed upper lip, which it uses to grab and pull food into its mouth, in the same way an elephant uses its trunk. Because of their distinctly different mouths, black and white rhinos are sometimes alternatively referred to as 'hook-lipped' and 'square-lipped' rhinos.

Unlike elephants, which tend to shred the ends of branches, black rhinos neatly shear off twigs using their molars, and crunch up the food, thorns and all. Characteristic neat pruning of woody vegetation is a sure sign of black rhino, quite different to the trail of destruction left by an elephant. Black rhino dung is also easily distinguished, containing fragments of leaves and twigs that are absent in white rhino dung, and more neatly clipped than in elephant dung.

The three Asian rhino species, like Africa's black rhino, also have prehensile upper lips. But the Indian one-horned rhino is predominantly a grazing animal, occupying an ecological niche closer to that of the white rhino than the black. It is a similar size to the white rhino, reaching 4850 lb (2200 kg) in males and 3530 lb (1600 kg) in females.

In India's Kaziranga National Park, where two thirds of the world's population of Indian one-horned rhino survive, they are often found feeding on short grass in the waterlogged meadows of the Brahmaputra floodplain. At night, and during the hottest part of the day, the rhinos retreat into the tall elephant grass that covers much of the area. In a network of tunnels worn through the 16 ft (5 meter) tall grass, the rhinos can shelter from the sun and sleep undisturbed.

Although short grass is its preferred food, the Indian one-horned rhino will also feed

Indian one-horned rhino calf, Kaziranga National Park, Assam.

on twigs and fruit in patches of dense forest, and on reeds and water plants, including carpets of water hyacinth which have invaded the shallow 'bheels' or swamps. When grazing is poor or rising floodwaters cover much of its range, the rhino may trespass on cultivated areas fringing the park, raiding crops.

The Indian one-horned rhino's smaller cousin, the Javan rhino, reaches a maximum weight of around 3000 lb (1400 kg) and is a mixed feeder, at times grazing in open grassy areas, but spending much more of its life in rainforest, feeding on leaves, young shoots, twigs and fallen fruit. It prefers areas of secondary growth, and will break down saplings to eat only from the crown. Although past distributions show that the Javan rhino is capable of adapting to varied environments, the tiny population remaining is now restricted to small areas of western Java and Vietnam. In Vietnam in particular the species has been pushed back into a marginal existence in bamboo and rattan thickets in steep, hilly terrain.

Sumatran rhinos are browsers, and are also very adaptable, occurring in habitats from sea level swamp to montane forest, although they prefer dense forest. Weighing no more than 2200 lb (1000 kg), the Sumatran species still needs to eat more than 110 lb (50 kg) of food a day. Its diet is made up of secondary plant growth, wild mangos, figs and bamboo. Once again man has eradicated this species from much of its former range in southeast Asia and the Himalayan foothills, and the isolated pockets which remain are often associated with high-altitude forest. Sumatran rhinos have been found as high as 10,825 ft (3300 meters), but this may be more a reflection of the need to avoid contact with man than a natural habitat preference.

An exclusively vegetarian diet does not always provide rhinos with all the nutrients they need, so they often consume mineral salts to supplement their diet. Where available, rhinos visit salt licks, sometimes using their horns to dig for minerals. Javan rhinos inhabiting the Ujung Kulon peninsula regularly drink seawater, while in Vietnam the species obtains salt from mineral springs.

Rhinos love wallowing – dried-on mud acts as a barrier to bloodsucking insects.

Given the opportunity, all rhinos will drink regularly. Rhinos sweat to cool off and need to replace the moisture they lose. In a well-watered habitat a white rhino will often drink twice a day and in captivity may drink up to 170 pints (80 liters) a day, but if water is distant a wild rhino may go without water for several days. Black rhinos will travel anything up to 15 miles (25 km) to waterholes and will dig for water in sandy riverbeds during droughts. They can get enough water from eating succulent plants to survive for up to four or five days without drinking if they have to. This adaptability has allowed black rhinos to survive in such arid environments as the desert of northern Namibia. In India and southeast Asia, rhinos migrate to lower-lying, moister areas in the dry season.

African and Asian rhinos share a fondness for wallowing in water and mud, and may spend hours partially submerged. Because rhinos are so plump, regulating their body temperatures can be difficult, so bathing and wallowing helps keep them cool. While rhinos generally feed most actively in the early and late parts of the day, they tend to wallow during the hottest time, rolling on their sides and backs to coat themselves in mud. Dried-on mud provides protection for their hairless skin against the sun, and local variations in soil color explain the wide variety of hide coloration seen in rhinos, from slate gray, through yellowish-browns, to vibrant, earthy oranges. A wet rhino appears almost jet black.

Mud also helps reduce moisture loss and most importantly acts as a barrier to irritating and potentially disease-bearing insects. Rhino skin may be tough, but it is well supplied with blood vessels and attracts blood-sucking ticks – hence the symbiotic relationship with birds like oxpeckers that enjoy feasting on these parasites. For those itches the oxpeckers can't relieve, rhinos can often be seen rubbing themselves against rocks or trees. Several different individuals from overlapping ranges will regularly use the same favorite rubbing post until it becomes as highly polished as a well-loved piece of furniture.

This old tree-stump is a favorite rubbing post for rhinos with unwanted ticks.

Social Organization

Turf Wars

It is dawn in the Zululand hills of South Africa, and a white rhino bull lumbers purposefully along a game path. He stops at a large pile of dung, sniffs, defecates, and then shuffles through the dung, scattering the pile with slow kicks of his hind legs. He moves on, pausing regularly to scrape the ground with his feet, leaving the distinctive smell of his dung behind. Further along the track, he side-swipes a small bush several times with his horn, before turning round and spraying it with a powerful jet of urine, another of his personalized calling cards.

Territorial male urine spraying.

The bull catches the scent of an intruder, another male rhino, perhaps a threat to his own territorial dominance. Head raised, ears cocked, he silently approaches the interloper, faces him horn to horn and stares. But this intruder is no threat, merely an adolescent male, known and tolerated by the dominant bull, and quick to show submission. Holding his head down, ears flat, the young male backs away, shrieking plaintively for mercy, until, at a safe distance, he turns and trots off. Satisfied that he has asserted his authority, the big bull resumes his patrol.

Territorial behavior is central to the social organization of rhinos. The popular belief that rhinos are solitary, antisocial animals tells only part of their story. African and Indian

Rhinos' large tubular ears swivel to pick up sound.

species can actually be quite sociable. Females and sub-adult African rhinos are rarely seen alone, and even dominant bulls will tolerate subordinate males within their domain.

White rhinos are the most sociable species, with the most complex social organization. Adult bulls, however, live a solitary existence, associating with females only when they are in estrus and meeting other males simply to dispute territories.

A dominant male holds a strictly defined territory, which he scent-marks by urine spraying along boundaries and by maintaining up to 30 dung heaps. The dung heaps, known as middens, are like large bulletin boards with a series of scented messages informing a passing rhino of who's around. A number of rhinos may use them, and they can be quite large, but only the territorial male scatters the dung by kicking.

The dominant bull will challenge any rhino he encounters on his turf. Such confrontations, often accompanied by noisy snorting, roaring and screaming, are dramatic to behold, but are largely ritualized and rarely result in actual violence. Eyeball-to-eyeball, the dominant male may bang horns with a subordinate male, and feign an attack. The subordinate rhino usually responds by adopting a submissive pose, backing away, and sometimes snarling or shrieking.

Because today most white rhinos live in fenced game parks where all available territory is occupied, normal dispersal of young male rhinos reaching adulthood is restricted. So young males must live an uneasy existence as subordinates within the territory of an established bull, sometimes their own father, until they are strong enough to take over a territory. Even then, their reign as dominant male may last only three years, before they too are overthrown and resume life as an older subordinate male, usually remaining on the same turf. But so long as a young male remains submissive, his presence will generally be tolerated. In fact a dominant male may allow more than one subordinate adult and several subordinate sub-adults to remain in his territory.

A trespassing stranger, on the other hand, receives a hostile reception, as the territorial bull rolls his eyes, flattens his ears, curls his lips and makes a shrill groaning

The white rhino's wide, square-lipped mouth is ideally suited for grazing.

sound. If this fails to warn off the interloper, the resident male will eventually charge, pursuing the fleeing stranger for up to a mile.

When two established territorial males meet at a border, they will stand horn to horn and stare at each other, occasionally backing off to swipe the ground, and sometimes mock charging. These stand-offs can last an hour, but despite the bluster usually both parties will eventually retreat, scent-mark, and wander off.

If a territorial male is caught trespassing in another's territory, perhaps on his way to a distant waterhole, he will usually allow himself to be shepherded back to the border. Outside his territory a bull acts like a subordinate and will not spray-urinate, but once he's back on home soil he resumes dominant behavior. Serious fights usually only occur when two males are competing for mating rights with a female, or when a male is attempting to take over a territory.

White rhinos readily use their horns as tossing and stabbing weapons against predators – quite a few safari vehicles have holes in their bodywork to prove it – but in disputes with other rhinos the horn is used more for sparring than stabbing. Serious puncture wounds are rare. The horn seems to be as much symbolic as it is practical, with a large, prominent horn acting as a signal of threat or dominance to pre-empt actual physical conflict. Behavioral signals such as ear posture also allow a weaker animal to indicate its capitulation so the dominant bull can allow it to flee without serious harm.

These visual signals are reinforced by vocal communication through a variety of rhino sounds. Some of them are quite incongruous for such a massive animal. Alarmed rhinos sometimes make an odd chirping sound when running away from danger and, just like children, sub-adults utter persistent whining noises to get what they want. Puffing and snorting loudly, fighting rhinos will grunt, groan and shriek like pigs.

Ritualized displays of dominance and submission largely allow rhinos to avoid serious injury or death, while the territory system reduces the likelihood of accidental confrontations. A badly injured rhino is vulnerable to predators such as lions, and because

Territorial black rhinos will drive away young adult males or even kill them.

rhinos are slow breeders, significant loss of life would be against the best interests of the species. However, as territory size is largely determined by availability of food and water, serious fights can become more frequent when population densities exceed the carrying capacity of the land – sometimes with fatal consequences.

Serious, occasionally deadly, fights are more common among black rhinos. Territorial black rhinos are much less tolerant of young adult males, and will drive them away or even kill them. Oddly, black rhinos can be surprisingly tolerant of neighboring territorial males. Unlike white rhinos, black rhino bulls may have overlapping territories. And for all their reputation as unpredictably excitable, two black rhino territorial bulls meeting on common ground will generally play out ritualized threat displays, then lose interest in one another. Sometimes they may even rest peacefully close by, or indulge in some gentle head butting.

Safeguarding an adequate food supply is one reason male rhinos defend their territory, but a more important motivation is to ensure there's little competition for the right to mate with resident females. One white rhino bull may have half a dozen or more mature female rhinos living within his territory. Adult females occupy quite small, overlapping ranges, which in good habitat may be less than 0.75 sq miles (2 sq km) in area. A female's territory may overlap with those of several males, and except when in estrus she can wander freely between them. However, when a dominant male does detect that a female is in estrus he will do his best to keep her within his territory, to ensure he alone gets the chance to mate with her.

White rhino cows are much more sociable than bulls, and are rarely seen alone. Typically a cow will be accompanied by her most recent calf, which stays with her until the age of two or three, when she calves again and drives it away. The rejected juvenile may then tag along with another cow and calf, or seek a companion of its own age.

Females tolerate other females and even seem to recognize one another, sometimes jostling horns half-heartedly when they meet. Two cows without calves may join up, and stable groups of four to six rhinos are often formed. Occasionally, larger collections of a dozen or more rhinos are seen, often at waterholes or salt licks, but these temporary groups soon drift apart. In South Africa's Hluhluwe-Umfolozi game reserve

*Waterholes and wallows are a good place to observe the often laid-back
social life of white rhino cows and their attendant calves on a hot day.*

one casual encounter we observed involved no fewer than 16 animals, including mothers with calves, several sub-adults, and a territorial male, busy smelling the urine of females to see if they were ready to mate. Female black rhinos, with or without calves, will also allow unrelated adolescents to accompany them and may sometimes form small groups, though not as commonly as the white rhino.

Unlike African rhinos, the Indian one-horned rhino is not truly territorial, though bulls do occupy poorly defined home ranges of up to 10 sq miles (25 sq km). Adult males sometimes form temporary groups of ten or more animals at wallows or on grazing grounds, happily tolerating one another. When confrontation between rival males does occur, display and posturing with curled lips and bared teeth are typical, but occasionally bluster and bluff escalate into noisy and prolonged fights. Indian rhinos have small horns but razor-sharp teeth, which can inflict serious, even fatal wounds.

White rhino cow and calf.

Both Javan and Sumatran rhinos tend to occupy large ranges. A female Javan rhino may have a range of up to 5 sq miles (13 sq km), and a male up to 8 sq miles (20 sq km). These ranges may overlap, but with populations often sparsely scattered over large areas bulls are also believed to wander widely on regular treks outside their home range, roaming vast distances to meet prospective mates.

Breeding

Rhinos are slow breeders, which can be a problem for conservationists trying to rebuild wild populations. Although a rhino can live for 50 years, females are slow to reach sexual maturity, have long gestation periods, and will only calve every two to four years.

For a female rhino maturity brings a cycle of breeding, gestation and motherhood. The age of sexual maturity for female rhinos varies between species, but is generally between four and eight years, with cows then going into estrus on a monthly cycle. Reproduction is a prolonged and hazardous experience, particularly for the male.

When a male rhino encounters a female within his territory he will attempt to smell her urine, which will enable him to tell if she is approaching estrus. But even approaching a female to urine-test is dangerous. At the best of times a rhino cow does not like a male rhino to come close and in estrus she becomes positively aggressive and defensive, especially if she has a young calf in tow. A cow will chase off the attentions of a bull with mock charges, and the bull must be cautiously persistent even to get close enough to test her urine, which he does with his head held high and mouth in a grimace.

When a rhino bull senses that a cow is approaching estrus, he must begin a patient and prolonged courtship, consorting with the cow for anything from three days to three weeks while she gets used to his presence. During this time he will keep a respectful distance, rarely being allowed closer than 15 ft (5 m). But if the cow appears to be wandering out of his territory he will block her way or chase her back with high-pitched squeals and wailing.

When the bull senses that a cow has come into full estrus, he will approach cautiously, perhaps swinging his head from side to side, huffing and snorting, but quick to retreat each time she threatens, until finally she allows him to rest his head on her rump and then attempt to mate. Eventually, after many hours of such approaches, the female will stand still and allow the male to mount her. Mating takes place in a standing position, with the bull's front feet placed over the cow's back, and lasts for about 30 minutes.

Although the pair rarely mate more than once, the bull may remain with the cow for several days afterwards, possibly to guard her against other males seeking an opportunity to mate. Unwanted attention from other males is a very real peril during mating – in India's Kaziranga National Park we observed a pair of one-horned rhino unable to complete copulation because of harrassment by another male. The mating bull had to dismount from the cow prematurely in order to chase away his rival.

Rhinos have a gestation period of around 15 to 16 months. When a cow is ready to calve she will seek dense cover, where she gives birth to a single calf, or in exceptional cases, two. A white rhino calf can weigh up to 140 lb (65 kg) at birth, stands about 20 in (50 cm) high, and already shows the first signs of its front horn. Although the calf can stand within ten minutes, it does not walk steadily for several days and the mother will keep it in cover for several weeks, before returning to her usual daily routine.

Young calves will begin grazing or browsing after two months, but are not weaned until after a year or more. The calves generally stay close by their mother, but they can be quite playful if they meet up with other calves, chasing around, practicing head-butting and horn wrestling. Cows separated from their calves call with a high, thin mewing, while a calf that has lost sight of its mother makes a panting sound to regain contact. A calf in distress will summon its mother or other nearby rhinos by squeaking.

Rhino bulls play no part in raising calves other than tolerating their presence within their territory. Where a bull holds onto his territory for many years he may well father several calves from each cow within that territory, but rhinos do not mate for life or remain faithful to specific partners. An individual cow is likely to have calves by several different bulls during her life, and indeed black rhino cows have been observed mating with more than one bull during a single eposide of estrus.

Although less is known about the behavior of the rare and elusive Javan and Sumatran rhinos they appear to lead more solitary lives than the African and Indian species, with adults only coming together to mate. The Sumatran rhino has something approaching a mating season, with most births occurring during the wettest months of October to May. Sumatran rhino calves are uniquely hairy when born, the hair turning a reddish brown in young adults, then becoming sparse and bristly and turning black in older animals.

This six-week-old white rhino calf has barely a bump for a horn.

A Deadly Trade

Rhinoceroses once roamed the plains and forests of Africa and Asia in their hundreds of thousands. Today they teeter on the brink of extinction. Even the relatively secure white rhino is restricted to a few heavily guarded strongholds. So what went wrong?

The rhino is a notable example of an animal that is disappearing faster that its habitat. Habitat loss is certainly a problem, but it is poaching for horn that is the most serious threat to all five species. Although man has hunted the rhino for thousands of years, for meat, for sport, and for body parts used in the manufacture of anything from drinking cups to armor, it is the modern trade in horn that has had the most devastating effect on the population. Two hundred years of unsustainable exploitation of wild rhinos, culminating in wholesale slaughter in the 1970s and 1980s as demand soared and supply declined, meant rhino horn literally became worth its weight in gold.

Trade in rhino horn began long before this, however, and was recorded in China as early as 2600 BC. Drinking cups made from rhino horn were highly prized for supposedly being able to detect poison. Improbable as it sounds, there may be some justification for the belief, as the alkaloids present in some poisons do react strongly with the keratin and gelatin in horn. Rhino skin was also used to fashion shields and armor, and, of course, the meat was eaten. Most significantly, horn and other body parts were regarded as powerful traditional medicines.

It is a popular misconception that rhino horn is used in the East mainly as an aphrodisiac. Although horn has certainly been used for this purpose, most notably in Gujarat and other parts of northern India, this was always a trivial market compared with other medicinal uses. Rhino horn, processed into pills, herbal treatments and tonics, is used to treat a wide range of serious ailments, including epilepsy, fevers, stroke, jaundice and AIDS. For practitioners of traditional Asian medicine, rhino horn is not perceived as a frivolous love potion, but as an irreplaceable pharmaceutical necessity.

Early signs of man's impact on rhino populations date back to the Chinese T'ang dynasty, between AD 600 and 900. A rapid expansion in eastern trade routes fueled demand for rhino products, and the Javan and Sumatran species went into decline. Rhinos were still widespread and common, however, when Europeans began exploring Africa and Asia. This was soon to change, as Western influence over land use and trade took effect.

Rhino habitat began disappearing rapidly under pressure from a fast-growing human population and the extensive conversion of land for agriculture. Much of the alluvial grassland of the Indian subcontinent vanished, and rhinos were killed as agricultural pests. Hunting for sport and horn reached unsustainable levels, with one maharajah alone killing 207 Indian rhinos in the late nineteenth century.

In Africa too, rhinos were hunted relentlessly. Kenyan game control officers clearing one area of land for agricultural use are said to have shot 1000 rhinos in two years. In the mid nineteenth century the southern white rhino was still so common that two hunters alone were able to kill 89 animals. By the beginning of the twentieth century only a handful of this subspecies survived.

Persecution and habitat destruction continued throughout the twentieth century, but it was in the 1970s that a serious new threat to rhino populations emerged from the Middle East. Rhino horn had traditionally been the favored material used to craft the handles of ceremonial daggers, called jambiyas, carried by the men of northern Yemen as status symbols. Carved rhino horn is lustrous, hard-wearing and develops a unique patina with age. Such expensive, high-status items were beyond the reach of most people until booming oil prices in the 1970s resulted in higher wages for Yemenis working in the Gulf and demand soared. The price of rhino horn rose 20-fold, with a devastating effect on African populations.

By the mid 1970s around 40 per cent of the world's trade in rhino horn was finding its way to Yemen. One major importer was bringing in 6600 lb (3000 kg) a year, representing the deaths of perhaps 1000 rhino. Another trader claimed to have imported over 79,000 lb (36,000 kg) in 16 years, a further 12,000 dead rhinos.

Meanwhile, trade in Asia was also booming. Rhino horn was imported through clearing houses in Hong Kong and Singapore to satisfy demand in the main markets of China, Taiwan and South Korea. In the early 1980s China alone was importing around

4400 lb (2000 kg) a year. Asian rhino populations had already crashed, so traders simply turned to cheaper African rhino imports.

Traditional medicine practitioners consider the 'fire horn' of Asian rhino species to be more potent than the 'water horn' of African rhinos, so it fetches a higher price. By 1990 the price of Asian horn had reached more than $20,000 per kilo, while African horn was in excess of $10,000. A single rhino horn could sell for as much as $80,000. Prices just kept rising. By the mid 1990s Asian rhino horn was fetching $60,000 per kilo.

International attempts to stem the trade, meanwhile, proved largely ineffective. In 1977 the Convention on Trade in Endangered Species (CITES) listed all rhino species on Appendix 1, prohibiting international commercial trade in their products. But with some consumer countries not even party to the agreement, and many states failing to implement their own domestic laws banning trade, global measures made little difference. Trade bans merely drove the trade underground and produced a further hike in prices.

Throughout the 1970s and 1980s few countries had adequate legislation to deal with rhino poaching. Key African range states were racked by civil wars, poverty and political corruption. Illegal poaching swept through Kenya, then Tanzania, Mozambique, Zambia and Zimbabwe. Uganda's black rhinos were decimated during the political unrest of the 1970s. In Mozambique, South African armed forces were complicit in illegal wildlife trade, while UNITA troops in Angola swapped rhino horn for weapons.

Automatic weaponry was readily available to poachers, who risked only trivial fines if caught. Although a poacher might receive $100 for a horn that would eventually sell for $30,000, the rewards were equivalent to two years' hard toil on the land and middlemen found no shortage of local people willing to take their chances, even where desperate game wardens adopted shoot-to-kill anti-poaching policies.

In parts of central Africa ill-trained, underequipped game guards were no match for heavily armed professional poaching gangs mounting cross-border raids. In India, poachers found ever more ingenious methods of killing rhinos, such as tapping into

Practitioners of traditional medicine believe Asian rhino horn is the most powerful.

overhead power lines to lay wires across regular rhino tracks and electrocute the unsuspecting animals. Between 1970 and the mid 1990s, over 90 per cent of the world's rhino population was wiped out. The black rhino population crashed from 100,000 in 1960 to 65,000 in 1970, then to around only 2500 by 1993. The northern white rhino population, which in 1960 probably outnumbered its southern cousin with around 2250 individuals, collapsed to a mere 11 animals in 1984. The Javan rhino hit a low of 20 to 30 animals in western Java in the 1960s, and the Indian rhino population fell to 750 in 1975.

This catastrophic decline meant conservationists had to try desperate measures to halt the slaughter. In Zimbabwe a controversial black rhino dehorning program was begun in 1993. Rhinos were darted and around three quarters of their front and rear horns was cut off by chainsaw or wood saw. Although researchers claimed no adverse effects were observed in the dehorned rhinos, the program was abandoned by the Zimbabwean Government in 1995, under fierce pressure from various wildlife lobby groups.

The late 1990s saw more encouraging signs. In Yemen, the government finally became a party to the CITES agreement and banned rhino horn imports and domestic trade. Although implementation was not totally successful, economic recession reduced the Yemenis' ability to afford rhino-horn dagger handles. Cheaper alternatives such as water buffalo horn and camel nails became acceptable, while agate and jasper emerged as expensive, high-status substitutes. International pressure also forced Asian states to enforce domestic legislation more vigorously. Japan, for example, which once imported 1700 lb (800 kg) a year of rhino horn, switched to using water buffalo and saiga antelope horn substitutes.

Nonetheless, investigations by TRAFFIC, the wildlife trade monitoring program of the Worldwide Fund for Nature (WWF) and the World Conservation Union (IUCN), revealed rhino horn medicines are still widely available in China, Taiwan, South Korea and Thailand, where huge stockpiles of horn have been built up. Taiwanese stocks were estimated at more than 9 tonnes in 1991, despite annual consumption averaging less than 1100 lb (500 kg). A 1998 registration of stocks held by Chinese medicine corporations revealed more than 10 tonnes of rhino horn, before taking into account retail outlets or privately owned material.

Registration of national rhino horn stockpiles was one of a number of new measures introduced by CITES in 1994. Recognizing earlier measures had failed to stem the decline in rhino numbers, CITES proposed a doubling of efforts to stop poaching and illegal trade. Uncritical reliance on legislative measures was no longer sufficient. Among the approaches suggested was a new emphasis on working together with traditional medicine practitioners to reduce demand.

Previously Western opinion scorned traditional medicine's use of rhino horn and failed to appreciate that practitioners valued it as a life-saving pharmaceutical rather than a means to turn a profit. These people saw little return from illicit trade anyway, with the big profits swallowed up by the organized traffickers. Traditional practitioners were insulted by the patronizing Western myth that rhino horn is used merely as an aphrodisiac, and felt trade bans forced them into illegal activity in order to provide an essential medicine. Few realized the impact the trade had on rhino stocks. By opening a constructive, dialog with traditional practitioners, organizations like TRAFFIC now hoped to encourage the use of substitutes for rhino horn.

For the future, law enforcement efforts are turning to modern technology to help fight the illegal trade. A major project to collect and analyze horn samples from different African populations has begun, with a view to setting up a database of chemical rhino horn 'fingerprints'. Horns accumulate chemical signatures from trace elements absorbed in a rhino's diet. Because these signatures appear to be unique to different home areas of rhino, investigators hope to use the database to trace the origins of confiscated horn, helping them identify illegal trade routes, produce evidence in court and warn parks that poaching is taking place.

In another application of technology, microchip transponders are being implanted into the horns and shoulders of rhinos that have been immobilized, for research, translocation or veterinary purposes. These will help in the identification of carcasses and the tracking of horn when rhinos are poached.

For the moment, poaching remains a problem throughout the remaining rhino ranges, albeit at a lower level than before. Rhinos have all but disappeared from the vast, open and virtually indefensible spaces they used to roam in Africa. Many of those that remain are in smaller, heavily guarded reserves making protection that bit easier. Civil unrest, political complacency, local corruption and diminishing conservation funds remain major problems, however.

In the Democratic Republic of Congo, what infrastructure was in place to protect the northern white rhino was largely looted or destroyed when conservation support staff had to abandon their posts during the civil war of the late 1990s. Miraculously, when they returned two dozen rhino had survived. In Zimbabwe, what remains of the country's black rhino population is seriously threatened by political unrest and land invasions. India's one-horned rhino stronghold, Kaziranga National Park, still sees up to 12 animals a year lost to poachers, while in Indonesia the thinly scattered population of Sumatran rhino living in dense, inaccessible rainforest makes protection against poaching almost impossible.

Habitat loss continues unchecked, particularly in southeast Asia. In Vietnam traditional slash-and-burn agriculture allowed forests to produce secondary growth that was attractive fodder for rhinos. Although the practice continues, crops of cashew nuts or mulberry are now planted, preventing regeneration. Uncontrolled logging and conversion of forest to farming has fragmented the ranges of Javan and Sumatran rhino. The few remaining rhinos are often in tiny isolated populations, which are too small to be genetically viable. Logging has destroyed the natural wildlife corridors which allowed rhinos to migrate between populations and find new mates, leaving those that survive vulnerable to inbreeding.

Back From the Brink

Two landmark successes in the story of rhino conservation prove it is possible to win the battle for their survival.

Visit the Hluhluwe-Umfolozi game reserve in KwaZulu-Natal, South Africa, and you could notch up sightings of white rhino into double figures on a single game drive. The parks of this South African state are among the best places in the world to see these lumbering megaherbivores at close quarters. But a hundred years ago, when the Umfolozi section of the park was first established, the sort of numbers you might now encounter during a short stay represented the only white rhino of the southern subspecies left on the planet. Numbers were down to around 20 animals. The situation was critical. Like the Sumatran and Javan rhinos today, these animals were staring extinction in the face.

The battle to protect this last surviving population of white rhinos and restore its numbers is one of the world's greatest conservation success stories. Although the foundations for this success were laid in 1895 when the Umfolozi park first gave these animals some effective protection, it was pioneering conservation work in the early 1960s that saw real progress. As well as building up rhino numbers through increased protection in the reserve, improved darting, game capture and translocation techniques made the successful reintroduction of rhinos to areas within their former range possible for the first time.

In 1961 park wardens began important work translocating rhinos. Sadly, the first rhino died during the process, but the now famous 'Operation Rhino' had begun. The techniques conservationists began perfecting were eventually to be used throughout the world. By 1972, 1109 white rhinos had been relocated to parks and reserves across Africa and to captive-breeding institutions around the world. By the year 2001 over 10,000 white rhinos had been translocated worldwide.

Today every southern white rhino you'll come across in the wild is descended from

White rhinos can be approached quite closely in key South African reserves.

this original Umfolozi population. From that small group there are now some 10,400 southern white rhino roaming the earth. Thanks to this long history of success South Africa has become a major player in rhino conservation. About 80 per cent of Africa's rhinos are located in the country.

In some areas numbers of white rhino are growing so rapidly that parks even have a surplus. Confined by fences and with pressure on space, game reserves can only support a limited number of animals. Those reserves with more animals than their carrying capacity face a difficult dilemma. Surplus animals have to be moved to other parks and game areas or it may eventually become necessary to carry out controlled culling, a controversial and obviously undesirable solution.

Conservationists in Africa, however, have found a novel alternative. It's a simple, practical solution that has succeeded, not only because it puts a 'conservation' value on the rhino's head, but also because it has the added bonus of providing further cash for rhino conservation. Surplus animals are sold at auction and the income generated is plowed back into protecting the species.

Every year for the last dozen or so years, one of the most unusual events on South Africa's wildlife calendar takes place, with much excitement and the usual media circus. Under a gaudy black and white marquee in the Hluhluwe-Umfolozi reserve, conservationists and game ranchers gather to take part in Africa's biggest and most prestigious game sale. Like every auction there is a catalog, viewing and an experienced auctioneer in charge of proceedings, but in this case the items under the hammer are live wild animals – and the star lots are the rhinos.

This annual sale can bring in around US$2.8 million and the income generated helps offset the management costs of important game reserves like Hluhluwe-Umfolozi. In 2001 revenue from the auction represented around 15 per cent of total annual income for KZN Wildlife Service, which runs South Africa's premier rhino reserves. The biggest slice of the income is derived from rhino sales. But if you are thinking of splashing out on a rhino, be warned. Black rhinos at the 2001 auction sold for over US$70,000 each, and buyers are strictly vetted. Most rhinos sold at the auction go to private game ranchers,

This black rhino (right), darted and captured
in Mhkuze game reserve, South Africa, by KZN Wildlife
Service's game capture team, is partially dehorned to
avoid injuring itself. The rhino was subsequently bought by
a private game rancher for a record $70,000 (£50,000)
at the annual KZN wildlife auction (above). The proceeds
from this unusual game sale are plowed back
into rhino conservation.

A one-month-old orphaned white rhino seeks reassurance by nuzzling his keeper's leg at the KZN Wildlife Service game capture bomas in the Hluhluwe-Umfolozi reserve. When he is old enough he too may be sold at the game auction.

who see rhinos as a major attraction for international tourists.

Each year around April time, rhinos to be sold at the auction are rounded up by expert game capture teams and experienced vets. It's a big operation that has to be carried out with skill and care to ensure the rhinos and those involved don't come to any harm. The teams work hard to ensure stress for the animals is kept to a minimum, but it's difficult work; rhinos are dangerous animals and even when sedated can be tricky to move because they are so big and heavy.

In the early days of 'Operation Rhino' there were worse problems with rhino capture. While it was possible to chase down other animals with vehicles and then use ropes and rangers to manhandle them to the ground, this clearly wouldn't work with rhinos. In the early 1960s conservationists began experimenting with tranquilizing drugs. The first attempts were not very successful and often the rhinos failed to respond to the drug combinations. It could take as long as 20 minutes for the drug to take effect and in the meantime the animal might have traveled as far as 5 miles (8 km). If a much larger dose was administered, on the other hand, the range of the dart was limited and the animal could be left with serious dart wounds.

In 1963 a new drug, M99, a derivative of morphine, revolutionized rhino capture. The animals could be tranquilized in 8 to 12 minutes and because doses were quite small dart wounds were no longer a problem. Back then rhinos were darted by game rangers on foot or on horseback, with the riders steering the darted animal so it didn't go off into thick bush before the drug did its work. Once the animal was down it could be restrained with a rope until the game truck arrived. At this point an antidote was injected into the rhino's ear so that it could be walked, still in a dazed state, for up to 2 miles (3 km) if need be, to the truck.

Since 1992 conservationists in KwaZulu-Natal have used helicopters in game capture. It is much easier to locate an animal from the air and darting can be done quickly and with a minimum of stress. A second, more powerful helicopter can then be guided to the darted animal to drop off a ground crew and cargo net. The rhino is dragged onto the net, which is then hoisted up by slings and airlifted straight to a game capture enclosure, or 'boma'. The rhinos are held here and monitored until their translocation or sale.

At first KZN Wildlife Service (then known as the Natal Parks Board) offered surplus rhinos for sale at relatively small sums to encourage buyers, particularly those from the private sector. Once the animals were allowed to realize their true market value, however, prices rose steadily. This has helped fuel the incentive to conserve and breed rhinos on South Africa's growing number of private game reserves.

Private sector involvement means that available habitat for rhinos has increased. Nowadays about 20 per cent of Africa's southern white rhinos have homes on South Africa's private reserves. There is even one group of privately owned white rhinos on a game reserve grazing on land that forms a buffer zone around an explosives factory!

Another benefit of the auction system is that conservation departments have been able to campaign for stiffer penalties for rhino crime simply because it's now possible to demonstrate the worth of a live rhino by pointing to the large sums of money they command. In recent cases maximum sentences of 10 years' imprisonment in South Africa, and 20 years in Namibia, have been handed down to poachers. Figures showing poaching levels to be generally on the decline at the end of the 1990s are giving rise to cautious optimism.

Another cause for optimism is the news that numbers of black rhino are also now starting to increase for the first time since records have been compiled. This rise is largely due to population increases in South Africa and Namibia, where numbers have risen by as much as 25 per cent.

While there's no room for complacency about such figures, the fact that small numbers of surplus black rhino are also now sold at the Hluhluwe auction is a far cry from the late 1930s when only two breeding populations of about 110 of these animals survived in South Africa.

Our second rhino conservation success story belongs to the Indian species, that

A white rhino in its holding pen before the game auction.

one-horned character with the unmistakable wrinkly hide. Despite its tough-looking exterior, this animal was extremely vulnerable in the early 1900s when its chances of survival were on a par with those of the southern white rhino. Something had to be done. In 1908 when Kaziranga National Park, in Assam, northeast India, was first declared a forest reserve, only a dozen or so Indian rhinos survived there.

There are now an estimated 2400 Indian one-horned rhinos in India and Nepal, with perhaps 1600 of these in Kaziranga. Populations in Nepal, which has also been successful in conserving them, are increasing at around 3.7 per cent a year and work to rebuild numbers elsewhere in the animal's former range is tentatively underway.

The fact that we can enjoy the thrilling experience of sitting astride an elephant, exchanging curious glances with a rhino just a few feet away is testimony to the hard work and dedication of game rangers in the field, the commitment of the Indian and Nepalese authorities and the vital support of the world's conservation agencies.

So how did they manage to do it? Underpinning the success of rhino conservation in India and Nepal, the high ratio of staff involved in anti-poaching procedures has been critical. Not long after Nepal's Royal Chitwan National Park was opened in the early 1970s, a contingent of the Royal Nepalese Army was called in to help combat poaching. It worked. Poaching within the park is now said to be almost unheard of.

It is estimated that one person per third of a square mile (1 sq km) is needed for conservation of this species to be effective. Although it might be difficult to argue for the same level of manpower to protect Javan and Sumatran rhinos, because of their dense rainforest habitat and sparse, widely scattered populations, successful rhino protection in the field is a heavy consumer of human resources. Even in Africa one field ranger for every 10 to 11½ sq miles (30 sq km) is considered necessary to carry out anti-poaching measures effectively. In Botswana, where very few rhinos remain, the national defense force has had to provide round-the-clock protection from watchtowers in one rhino sanctuary. Today in Kaziranga groups of forest guards man observation towers and

Indian rhinos occupy home ranges of 4 to 10 sq miles (10 to 25 sq km).

59

anti-poaching stations from where they make regular patrols of the parks and continual checks on the rhinos.

In the 1970s and 1980s a combination of photo registration and counting techniques was used to establish numbers and monitor the Indian rhino population in Chitwan. Ecological studies in the reserve to build up a database on the rhino population have been another key factor in the Indian rhino's recovery. The work has proved invaluable in providing data on the age and sex of animals and their home ranges. This not only helps management of the rhinos in the field, but allows conservation authorities to select the most suitable animals for translocation.

Of course this does not mean the Indian one-horned rhino is out of the woods yet. The many opportunities that exist for further translocations and improved ecological management techniques now need to be exploited. Poaching remains a significant threat to this species and expanding rural communities on the edge of rhino protection areas continue to push at park boundaries for space to graze their animals and grow crops. Annual flooding of preferred rhino habitat close to water sources also regularly claims the lives of these animals. And there is always the question of where tomorrow's funding to adequately equip forest guards and anti-poaching patrols will come from.

The preservation of all five rhino species depends on the successful resolution of many outstanding issues in a complex conservation puzzle. If new plans to rebuild rhino numbers in their natural habitat are to succeed we need to ensure sufficient habitat remains available and is maintained and improved.

While there may now be safety in numbers for the African rhino beloved by tourists on safari in South Africa's Zululand reserves, it would be premature to close the book on their story just yet. Conservationists may have found a way to supplement the cost of rhino conservation just in time. The prospect of declining government budgets for future conservation work means the fight to safeguard these rhinos goes on.

The white rhino is the more placid of the two African species.

A Future In Question

At the start of the twenty-first century, conservationists are pinning their hopes on some tough new measures to save the threatened rhino species from extinction. Plans to rescue the rare western subspecies of black rhino, for example, by assigning each animal its own personal bodyguard, might seem a little extreme, but drastic steps like these are needed in an emergency.

In Cameroon, west Africa, the race is on to create an intensively protected and managed sanctuary in the wild. There are believed to be fewer than 15 western black rhino left, against the 20 animals considered necessary to form a 'founder population' from which numbers can be restored. Any rhino group of fewer than 10 animals is at grave risk of extinction, even when conditions are good. To have any hope of success, conservationists need to work from a base group of at least three female and two male rhinos in a location that's safe from poachers. Their initial target is a population of 50 animals by the year 2050.

Rhino conservation specialists are setting considerable store for the rhino's future in the creation of 'wild' sanctuaries like this, where funds and personnel are concentrated in relatively small areas. A similar concept in Kenya has proved successful in conserving African black rhino. The idea is now being adapted to rescue Sumatran and Javan rhinos.

Not so long ago Asian rhino conservation efforts placed considerable emphasis on captive breeding programs in zoos, but results were disappointing. Indian rhinos appeared to breed quite happily in zoos, but between 1984 and 1995 half of the 40 Sumatran rhinos involved in captive breeding projects died, without a single successful captive birth.

Now the focus is switching towards breeding Asian rhinos in their native habitats, using core protection zones, similar to some of the sanctuaries that have proved successful in Africa. A number of captive Sumatran rhinos have already been repatriated to live semi-wild in closely guarded enclosures in prime rhino habitat. It is hoped managed breeding undertaken in the 'virtual wild' will bring about the long

Rhinos are heading into an uncertain future unless conservation measures are stepped up.

hoped-for reversal in the fortunes of these rhinos.

At Way Kambas in southeast Sumatra conservationists are hard at work to realize this vision. A 250 acre (100 ha) sanctuary within the park, protected by an electric fence, has been created by the International Rhino Foundation and the Indonesian government. It is hoped that from a handful of rhinos a new dynasty of Sumatran rhinos will emerge.

The new-style Asian rhino sanctuaries are smaller and more actively managed than their African counterparts. In Africa, choosing a mate is left to the rhinos, but in these new, managed breeding centers it is conservationists who will select the right breeding partners from the available gene pool. If successful, it is hoped these sanctuaries will evolve along African lines, protected areas will be expanded and the choice of mate will once again be restored to the rhinos. Underpinning the success of such ventures, however, is the need to step up anti-poaching measures and increase the number of rhino protection units to ensure these special breeding populations remain secure.

Ultimately such projects aim to establish viable wild populations of all three Asian species. How many rhinos do we need for this to happen? With only a small rhino population in any one area, the danger is that poaching or disease could easily wipe out all the animals. This was all too clearly illustrated when five Javan rhinos in Ujung Kulon National Park in western Java were lost to an unidentified virus. In order to increase long-term chances of survival, therefore, several populations of at least 100 rhino each are considered desirable for each species. Long-term viability would require between 2000 and 3000 of each rhino species in the wild.

Such measures cost money. Although a cost-effectiveness study carried out a few years ago identified intensive protection zones as one of the most successful methods of conserving rhinos, rhino conservation is not cheap. 'Where will the money come from?' and 'Will the funding dry up?' are questions that trouble every rhino conservationist.

Building the planned 104 sq mile (270 sq km) sanctuary to safeguard Cameroon's western black rhino, for example, will cost around US$1.5 million over five years. The total amount required to finance conservation strategies for Asian rhinos in the years from 1996 to 2000 was calculated to be about US$33 million. In South Africa in a park of 195 sq miles (500 sq km) it is estimated that at least US$1000 per square kilometer is needed for adequate rhino protection. In other areas this figure may be nearer US$1400.

The Worldwide Fund for Nature (WWF) alone has given US$13 million to rhino protection projects in the years between 1961 and 1994. But despite the continued efforts of such key donor agencies, there has always been a bigger demand than supply when it comes to hard cash for conservation.

One survey by TRAFFIC of 18 countries that were not home to rhinos found only five had provided funding to help them. Historically, less than one third of the money needed for rhino conservation has actually been available, according to the Asian and African specialist rhino groups of the IUCN, the world conservation union.

Since the late 1970s these two specialist groups have undertaken a vital role as the rhinos' advocates. Through the development of comprehensive conservation 'action plans' for all five rhino species, they

Roadside conservation message in Assam.

have pressed for a more coordinated approach to rhino protection. Clearly defined conservation objectives help direct efforts and resources to where they are needed most and where there is the biggest chance of success.

Both groups stress that in future rhino conservation needs to be more financially self-sufficient than it is today. In a world where poorer countries must weigh the demand of their human populations for scant resources against the conservation of wildlife, we are already starting to see cutbacks in conservation budgets. Conservationists argue that finding ways to generate self-sustaining income for rhino conservation from enterprises such as eco-tourism is becoming more and more imperative.

Some of the ideas being discussed to help make rhino conservation pay its way are controversial. In South Africa, for example, limited sport hunting of surplus male white rhinos to help fund conservation efforts has been allowed for some time. Even more radical is a proposal for a limited and controlled legal trade in rhino products. With numbers of white rhino having the potential to double in the next decade, the argument goes that legalized trade could produce both the revenue and incentives needed for long-term self-sufficiency in the funding of rhino conservation.

Less contentious is the need to convince poor communities living close to rhino protection areas that conservation is a worthwhile activity. Where local people are given a vested interest in rhino conservation and are allowed to partake in the economic benefits, the chance of long-term security for the rhinos is likely to increase.

The WWF's community game guards and rural community project in Kaokoland and Damaraland, Namibia, have demonstrated how the knowledge and experience of local people can be harnessed to help in both species and habitat management. As well as local families making a living from the scheme, the use of community game guards has proved effective in helping to reduce poaching.

In another example, all tourists visiting the Hluhluwe-Umfolozi reserve now pay a 'community levy' that goes directly to the local Zululand people. Conservation authorities allow local people controlled access to this reserve to harvest natural resources such as thatching grass and encourage them to grow and sell vegetables to the reserve's restaurant and run craft stalls selling souvenirs to tourists. With a stake in the 'end product', local people have a positive reason to ensure the rhino's future is secured.

If we are to have any real chance of winning the race against extinction, the illegal trade in rhino horn and rhino products must stop. After everything else has been said and done, this is still our best hope of saving some of our planet's most charismatic creatures for the generations that follow us.

To save these charismatic creatures we need to end the illegal trade in horn.

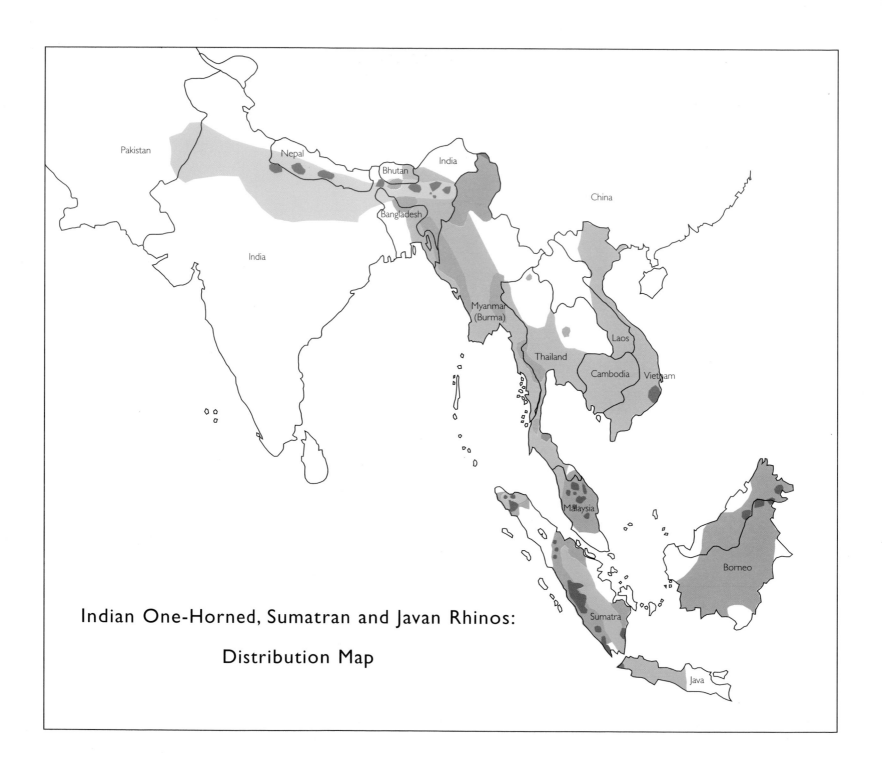

Pakistan

Nepal

Bhutan

India

China

Bangladesh

India

Myanmar
(Burma)

Laos

Thailand

Cambodia

Vietnam

Malaysia

Borneo

Sumatra

Java

Indian One-Horned, Sumatran and Javan Rhinos:

Distribution Map

Asian Rhino Facts

Indian Rhino

Past Distribution
c. 1800

Present Distribution

Scientific name: *Rhinoceros unicornis*
Estimated wild population*: 2400
Common names: Indian or Nepalese
rhino, Asian greater one-horned rhino
Weight: 3500 – 6000 lb
(1600 – 2700 kg)
Shoulder height: 60 – 72 in
(150 – 185 cm)
Head and body length: 120 – 150 in
(300 – 380 cm)
Horns: One, up to 24 in (60 cm)
Habitat: Riverine grasslands and
floodplains
Age at maturity: Females 5 – 7 years,
                 Males 10 years
Gestation period: 15 – 16 months
Longevity: 47 years
(recorded in captivity)

Sumatran Rhino

Past Distribution
c.1800

Present Distribution
Tiny, isolated populations
may still exist elsewhere in
historic range, but reports
are unconfirmed.

Scientific name: *Dicerorhinus sumatrensis*
Estimated wild population*: 300
Common names: Sumatran rhino,
Asian two-horned rhino, hairy rhino
Weight: 1300 – 2200 lb
(600 – 1000 kg)
Shoulder height: 44 – 57 in
(110 – 145 cm)
Head and body length: 90 – 125 in
(235 – 320 cm)
Horns: Two, largest up to 30 in (74 cm)
Habitat: Tropical rainforest and
mountain forest
Age at maturity: 7 – 8 years
Gestation period: 17 months
Longevity: 32 years

Javan Rhino

Past Distribution
c.1800

Present Distribution

Scientific name: *Rhinoceros sondaicus*
Estimated wild population*: 60
Common names: Javan rhino,
Asian lesser one-horned rhino
Weight: 2000 – 3000 lb
(900 – 1400 kg)
Shoulder height: 62 – 70 in
(160 – 175 cm)
Head and body length: 120 – 125 in
(300 – 320 cm)
Horns: One, up to 10 in (25 cm)
Habitat: Lowland tropical rainforest
Age at maturity: Females 3 – 4 years,
                 Males 6 years
Gestation period: 16 months
Longevity: 35 – 40 years

*Source: Population figures for all rhino species from
IUCN/SSC African and Asian Rhino Specialist Groups and the International Rhino Foundation.

African Rhinos: Distribution Maps and Facts

African White Rhino

Scientific name: *Ceratotherium simum*
Estimated wild population*: 10,400
Common names: African white rhino, wide-lipped rhino, square-lipped rhino
Weight: 3000 – 6600 lb (1400 – 3000 kg)
Shoulder height: 60 – 72 in (150 – 180 cm)
Head and body length: 130 – 165 in (335 – 420 cm)
Horns: Two, largest up to 60 in (150 cm)
Habitat: African savannah, long and short grass
Age at maturity: Females 6 – 7 years, Males 10 – 12 years
Gestation period: 16 months
Longevity: 40 – 60 years

Past Distribution c.1800

Northern White Rhino

Southern White Rhino

Present Distribution

Please note that very small scattered populations reintroduced to game farms are not shown.

African Black Rhino

Scientific name: *Diceros bicornis*
Estimated wild population*: 2700
Common names: African black rhino, hook-lipped rhino
Weight: 1750 – 3,000 lb (800 – 1,400 kg)
Shoulder height: 55 – 70 in (40 – 180 cm)
Head and body length: 120 – 150 in (300 – 375 cm)
Horns: Two, largest up to 50 in (130 cm)
Habitat: Tropical bushland, grassland and savannah in Africa
Age at maturity: Females 4 – 7 years, Males 7 – 10 years
Gestation period: 15 to 16 months
Longevity: 45 – 50 years

Past Distribution c.1800

Black Rhino

Present Distribution

Please note that information on present distribution is often unreliable, or partially suppressed for security reasons. Locations shown are approximate.

Recommended Reading

Despite the rhino's high profile, there are surprisingly few books in print on this animal.

The Behavior Guide to African Mammals, by Richard Estes (University of California Press, 1991) is an accessible, well-documented book with a chapter devoted to the behavior and biology of the two African rhino species. Also available in paperback, this is a useful book to take into the field on safari.

The Complete Book of Southern African Mammals, edited by Gus Mills with photography by Lex Hes (Struik, 1997). This book is large in size and scope and contains good, concise descriptions of the behavior, habitat and biology of both African species.

The African Rhino Specialist Group Action Plan, by Richard Emslie and Martin Brooks (IUCN, 1999) and *The Asian Rhino Specialist Group Action Plan*, edited by T.J. Foose and Nico van Strien (IUCN, 1997), provide excellent, in-depth summaries of the current status of the five remaining rhino species and the conservation measures required to protect them. Contact the IUCN Publication Services Unit, 219c Huntingdon Road, Cambridge CB2 0DL, UK.

Horn of Darkness: Rhino on the Edge, by Carol Cunningham and Joel Berger, (Oxford University Press Inc, USA, 1997) tells the story of attempts to conserve the black rhino, with a blend of natural history and first-hand experience.

Biographical Note

Ann and Steve Toon travel thousands of miles each year to photograph the world's wildlife. They spend as much time as possible in the field documenting the natural behavior of wild subjects and the work of conservationists. Based in northwest England, on the edge of the Lake District, they have come to regard the game parks of Southern Africa as a second home, but also work regularly on location in Australia, India and southeast Asia. They also enjoy photographing the wildlife of Britain. Ann and Steve have an extensive background in journalism and write regularly for magazines and newspapers on natural history, photography and ecotourism.

Index

*Entries in **bold** indicate pictures*

Useful Contacts

For more information or to contribute to rhino conservation the following organizations are worth contacting:

The International Rhino Foundation (IRF)
c/o The Wilds
14000 International Road
Cumberland
Ohio 43732
USA
www.rhinos-irf.org

The IUCN African Rhino Specialist Group
KZN Wildlife Service
PO Box 13053
Cascades
3202
South Africa
www.iucn.org

The IUCN Asian Rhino Specialist Group
No 10. Jalan Bomoh
off Jalan Keramat
Hujong
54200 Kuala Lumpur
Malaysia
www.iucn.org

Worldwide Fund for Nature (UK)
Panda House
Weyside Park
Catteshall Lane
Godalming
Surrey
GU7 1XR
www.wwf.org

World Wildlife Fund (USA)
1250 24th Street N.W.
Washington, DC 20037
USA
www.worldwildlife.org

Save the Rhino International
16 Winchester Walk
London
SE1 9AQ
www.savetherhino.org